# LETTERS FROM LILLIAN

*From Her Heavenly Home to My Heart*

# LETTERS FROM LILLIAN
*From Her Heavenly Home to My Heart*

DR. LEE TOMS

Pascoe Publishing, Inc.
Rocklin, California

Cover and page design by Vanessa Perez Design

Published in the United States of America by
Pascoe Publishing, Inc.
Rocklin, California
http://www.pascoepublishing.com

ISBN: 1-929862-36-9

04   05   10   9   8   7   6   5   4   3   2   1

Printed in China

# Letters From Lillian

These letters lay no claim to Heavenly correspondence nor to spiritual dictation. They are simply the product of my own heart, albeit a heart so deeply blended with the heart of another that the two hearts seem to beat as one. Though the letters are self-written, they have seemed strangely comforting as though they were the true product of her own loving heart. Someday no such imagined communication will be necessary when at last we can tell each other all our hearts' deepest thoughts, when all separation is at last put behind us and the future stretches endlessly before us. Until then, these heartfelt messages must suffice. The basis of the hopes expressed are facts as revealed by the Father in His word and to my searching heart.

For the privilege of knowing Lillian and loving her, I am eternally grateful to the Father whose gift of love she was and is and ever shall be. Lillian was a precious gift of God to me, of whom I was undeserving and unworthy. When but fifteen I met and fell in love with a pretty young girl of fourteen, I never dreamed what a totally beautiful gift she would become nor what a priceless treasure to my heart and life. For fifty-two years of marriage and fifty years of partnership in gospel ministry she influenced, impacted and inspired my life. She was a gracious and godly person and left indelible fingerprints all over my heart. Her sudden and wholly unexpected departure for her Heavenly home left me lonely for her and longing to rejoin her. This separation phase of our lives and our love is neither complete nor permanent. Life and love from God and in Christ are indeed stronger than death.

> "Death can hide but not divide
> Thou art but on Christ's other side
> Thou with Him and He with me
> United still in Christ are we."

(author unknown)

## Dearest Lee,

Today, June 5, 2002, marks our fifty-third wedding anniversary, our first ever apart. When we married we promised "till death do us part, and as long as we both shall live." We are both still very much alive. I am gone from your sight, but I live in an upper room of our Father's house. Our Father's gentle removal of me bodily did not end our God-ordained union; it only entered a new and unfamiliar phase. It was the Lord who joined us together as one fifty-three years ago when He created a mysterious but marvelous unity no man nor even the last enemy can tear asunder. Our love from God and in Christ endures never to be extinguished but enhanced and exalted. Today, along with you, I gratefully mark the sacred bond of holy matrimony that exists between us. Lee, what a fulfilling life is ours.

You do not celebrate this anniversary alone. Our life and love connect us unbreakably. My spirit joins with your spirit today, and we will rejoice together. We were and are God's perfect choice for each other. The years have only confirmed the confidence in which our love began. In the future that choice will be continued, completed and crowned.

Happy Anniversary, Dear
Love Always,
Lillian

*Happy Anniversa*

*never go back*

## Dearest Lee,

As you traveled today to your preaching assignment, I felt constrained to remind you of what we often said to one another on certain occasions in our travels, "Never go back." We cannot go back now; therefore we must simply go on as before. It truly is better farther on. If you do go back in memory or revisit places that tell of past joys, just remember I was with you in all of them. We made the memories together. We were privileged to share in the pleasures and enjoyment of many happy yesterdays. Let us pause together to thank God for all of them, and then we can go on to the unimaginably "better" that is before us. Our love will grow in this temporary separation and this absence will only make the expected reunion more precious to us both. I am with you today and you will feel the touch of my spirit upon yours until we meet to be separated never more.

Love Always,
Lillian

## Dearest Lee,

Please don't grieve for me even though I know it is an expression of love. Be thankful with me, rejoice with me, praise our gracious Lord with me for all we've known and shared and for the promised fulfillment to come. When you grieve I can't join you for all is peace and joy here. But when you praise, rejoice, give thanks, I am with you; we are together once more.

Love Always,
Lillian

*give thanks*

## Dearest Lee,

I know how much you miss me in my accustomed place as you preach His Word. For so many years I was always there to pray for you and support your labors for Him. You were my pastor as well as my life's partner. Do not for a moment think that I am not with you now, an unseen but not unreal presence, praying for you and encouraging you as always. Be heartened, dear, in all you do for Him; I am so pleased and rejoice in your labors as partners in service for Christ. Keep on keeping on. It pleases Him and it pleases me.

Love Always,
Lillian

*life partner*

*memory of us*

## Dearest Lee,

When the memories of our life together and its happiness bring you pain, please try to praise Him as I do, for the rare privilege and sweet pleasure we had in the making of those memories. They will never be erased from the memory of either of us. How very full our years were of love and joy and beauty. We were not just together; we were together "in Christ." That togetherness cannot be severed by our separation now. You have been left to deal not only with memories, but also with numerous reminders that surround you of former days, the "things" gathered over a married lifetime. They were not essential to us then or now; they are only the accessories of living. They are but trinkets in a life based on loving and sharing. Let them go, Lee. They have served their temporal purpose. Our true treasures are here to be enjoyed together forever.

Love Always,
Lillian

*love, our love*

## Dearest Lee,

It was just one year ago today that our Heavenly Father in wisdom and loving kindness gently removed me from you and brought me home. I am not conscious of time, but for you it has been a long and lonely year. Today, dear, on this anniversary of my separation from you, do not dwell on the time spent without me but think of the time you will spend with me. Your momentary affliction may seem long, but it is not possible to compare it with this eternal weight of glory. As always, I understand the wistfulness that pervades your life. The longing and yearning "to be with" is mine as well as yours. Just as life did not end for me but continues vibrantly and victoriously; so did love, our love. It was not cancelled upon entrance here, only enhanced and encouraged in this place where love reigns. One year ago today for you, but one year nearer home and unimaginable reunion for us both.

I've been wanting to tell you for some time that sixty years ago when we were "oh-so-young," you captured my heart and never let it go. It has always belonged to you and does now; the bond is ever tighter. It will never come untied.

Love Always,
Lillian

## Dearest Lee,

I know that it has been hard for you to visit the little cemetery in Fair Oaks. I was with you there today and rejoiced to hear you pray as you always do at that spot, thanking the Father that I was not there, never had been there, never will be there. The body that is there will be raised in power, honor, and beauty. I am more alive than ever, mortality is swallowed up of life. I am happily with the Lord, not in the ground. I read the note left by my dear son Dave on my birthday, which read "Happy Birthday, Mom. I love you." Please assure him my birthday was like no other, free of pain and care and tears. Tell him that I love him and all my children dearly, and that my prayers of many years continue here, that the circle will be unbroken in Christ and that at the end of life's day all of them will be safely home before dark.

Love Always,
Lillian

*r and beauty*

## Dearest Lee,

You always so lovingly said that next to the gift of eternal life I was the Lord's most precious gift to you. I loved to think of myself that way, as your heart's most cherished treasure. Please never think that this precious gift is lost to you. He has gently assured me that His gifts and callings are without any change of mind on His part. There is no power strong enough to take away from us what He has been pleased to bestow in love. I am not taken from you either fully (only in body and out of sight) or finally. Your gift is being kept in trust, safe and secure until the day when the gracious Giver will return the gift more precious than before. In the giving He has always intended the gift to be permanent, not temporary.

Love Always,
Lillian

*cherished treasure*

# *hope is ours*

## Dearest Lee,

All is wonderfully well. Healing there is only temporary. Healing here is permanent. Some hurts will only be healed in Heaven. I will never hurt again. No more painful and aching hips with every step. No more a heart running wildly and wondering when it will stop hurting or just stop. No more sleepless nights. All hurts are healed, all broken things are mended. The old Puritan said when dying, "I'm almost well." The almost for me is now all well. One hurt will be healed for us both when that which God Himself joined together, and which was partially torn asunder with my homecoming, is rejoined to be separated never more. What a prospect and what a hope is ours.

Love Always,
Lillian

## Dearest Lee,

Love that is of Divine appointment and Divine approval such as ours has both revelation and reason to testify that this love is a love in anticipation and does not end in grief and a grave. We experienced love's ascent during our life together. It had reached its highest and dearest meaning at the time of parting. Surely love's ascent does not come crashing down in ruins just as it reaches its highest point. To believe so is to make a mockery of love. The marvel and mystery of the two-made-one is destined for a greater marvel and mystery yet. For our two hearts which are fully in tune, it will mean these same two hearts fully in love's triumph.

Love Always,
Lillian

*greater marvel*

*hearts and lives*

## Dearest Lee,

You and I are no strangers to separation. Remember that most of the years between our meeting when love began and our marrying, were spent by necessity, apart from one another except for a few brief days each year. We were for the most part separated by hundreds of miles but never separated in mind or heart, and eager for the short time of happy reunion. Perhaps some way in our Father's plan He was preparing us for this present absence from each other. Out of sight temporarily, the same love that spanned the miles then, somehow bridges the distance now. As Paul said concerning his beloved Thessalonian brothers "...having been taken away from you for a short while in person, not in spirit, were all the more eager with great desire to see your face." Is not our absence but for a short while; isn't it only in person but never in spirit? Are we not the more eager with a great desire to see each other's face?

Love Always,
Lillian

## Dearest Lee,

*loving reunion*

During the periods of long separation in love's beginning for us, you looked at my picture and knew there was a real person in a certain place far removed from your sight. You knew that I was thinking of you, loving you, and waiting for the day when it would not be a picture but me that you would see. When you look at my picture now, which often causes you tears from memories and longing, just remember, dear, it is now as then. I am gone from you in presence, but even in absence one from another, we are together in heart and spirit, that unbreakable God-sanctioned bond. We shall meet again face to face and the pictures and memories will be needed no more. I am out of your sight for now but never out of your life. I am part of you and you of me forever. Those long ago long periods of separation eventually ended in a loving union of two hearts and lives. This separation shall end as well in a loving reunion of two hearts.

Love Always,
Lillian

*harmo*

## Dearest Lee,

Today in your visit to Portland, Oregon, you drove by the very street where so many years ago you asked me to be your wife. How surely did our Heavenly Father prompt the asking and how surely did He direct the answer. How could we have possibly known then of the years of harmony and happiness to which this commitment would lead us? Our Lord set our feet upon an unknown path but became our unfailing guide through the ensuing years. I am so grateful that you asked and that my answer pleased you as much as it pleased me to give it. We have told each other we would gladly do it again a hundred times over with never a serious regret. The love placed in us by a divine hand weathered all the storms, savored all the joys, bore all the pain, gained depth and meaning and learned the precious meaning of "oneness." That which began with two so young with a confidence in God's choice, lived through the years in covenant companionship and came reluctantly to the parting of our ways for a season. But that which began on a shaded street in Oregon with a simple but sincere question and its equally sincere answer, lives beyond life's fleeting years to be faithfully continued later in God's immeasurable grace and enduring kindness.

Love Always,
Lillian

*and happiness*

## Dearest Lee,

I do understand the heart hesitancy to return to the "Firs," that place of familiar scenes and sacred memories. It was there we felt the youthful beginning of a lifetime of love. Let our gentle Lord touch the tender emotions with tokens of His love, and the source of ours. If tears should fall, let them be tears of gratitude. I will be with you there truly and together we will pause and thank the Father for His wonderfully perfect plan for us. The seeds of love were planted then which were to bear a rich harvest of a fulfilling life together. Our first unsteady steps in a long and loving journey were taken there. How much poorer would our lives have been had not He made it clear to each of us "there could never be any other." Our Father blessed the beginning and prepared lovingly the unknown way ahead. What began there on the Bible conference grounds sixty years ago continues even now and will be wonderfully completed in this place He has prepared for us. A God-given love cannot be lost. At the "Firs" I waited often for you by our special tree in that distant past when we were young, and I wait for you now and the desired together will not be hours, days, or years, but forever.

Love Always,
Lillian

*seeds of love*

*spirit and heart*

## Dearest Lee,

This Heavenly life is knowing, rejoicing, remembering, loving. Forgetting what we had together is impossible; it is a matter for praise and gratitude here with the Lord. Loving you has been only intensified, not eliminated. I also know what is in store for us when He perfects and completes what He so graciously began and this is the source of great joy for me as I hope it is for you. What we had from the Father's hand on earth was but a foretaste and preview of what is to be experienced in due time. That hope is yours and that hope is mine as well. We will wait together in spirit and heart until waiting is over and separation will be no more. We will love each other more truly, more intensely, more unselfishly than ever. He has much more for us than we have ever known. Believe it fully, for there will be no disappointment. The foretaste of love was beautiful, what must the full taste be!

Love Always,
Lillian

# Dearest Lee,

Aren't we supremely grateful that a loving Lord has written our love story? He loved us and gave His Son for us in order to make possible the indispensable gift of eternal life. In loving guidance He brought us together in youthful love. Even during long months of separation He preserved our love and prompted its growth. He lovingly joined us in the bonds of love and graced our "oneness" of heart and life with His goodness and loving kindness. When the loving hand that gave us to each other separated us temporarily when I departed for home, He assured us that "bereft" of each other in person our love was not severed. How true it is that "we loved, we love, we will love." Our love story's last chapter remains to be written in the "gain" and the "far better" of His pledge and promises. He wrote the commencement of our story in love, and He will complete it in the same love. Because it is His story written in two hearts it will end tenderly, triumphantly and endlessly. In this interim just continue to love me as I do you. Our story that love wrote is to be continued and will surely have a Heavenly sequel.

Love Always,
Lillian

*loving guidance*

*pefectly fulfilled*

## Dearest Lee,

For a time before my departure from you, I expressed several times in notes to others that I had been forgiven, my life was perfectly fulfilled, and I was prepared for the Lord to call me home. At home with the Lord is now my place—happy and secure. You are surely remembered with a love made fuller and richer. You do not feel at home in the world anymore nor are you yet here in your heart's true home. The feeling of being "homeless" is surely real and painful. It won't be long, dear, but in the expecting, waiting time you will find a safe and satisfying home in the Lord Jesus. You at home in Him and I at home with Him. The closer you draw to Him, the closer you are to me. He has gracious and kind plans for you and me. Trust Him for all, for He will complete what He began, and it will last forever.

Love Always,
Lillian

*ever shall be*

## Dearest Lee,

This weekend you will be speaking at a couples conference and be among "twos." You will feel wistfully that you are but one and alone. The aloneness that you feel must include me, for our Lord mysteriously but marvelously took the two of us and created a wonderful oneness in body, mind, heart, spirit, and soul. The couples there are together in a sharing of life and love. Our togetherness in His life and His love was not severed by my departure. I did not get to tell you so suddenly did I leave you, but remember always I shall continually be with you. When mail comes to our house still addressed to Lee and Lillian, please don't let it trouble you but consider it as a testimony to what is graciously true; it is still Lee and Lillian and ever shall be.

Love Always,
Lillian

## Dearest Lee,

You may long for the days now gone, the healthy and happy days. The days before the marks of aging and illness began to appear. Those days are clearly defined and wondrously familiar while the coming days for you do not appear as clearly. You may feel that while you would confidently return to the known, you cannot face as confidently the largely unknown. All is well, Lee. All is graciously and lovingly all right. We truly enjoyed one another then and in some true if totally different way we can enjoy one another now. Be confident, dear, about tomorrow. We shall know each other better, love each other more, delight in each other fully. Unimaginably better than our past together will be our future together. Let all the past be a wonderful prophecy of what is to come and that without end.

Love Always,
Lillian

*future together*

## Dearest Lee,

Please do not wonder if memory has failed. I remember all, and the remembering here only contributes to my joy. You are remembered so thankfully and hopefully. Do not wonder if my love for you has ceased. It has grown and it is true that not only is His life stronger than death but His love is stronger than death. It was His life and His love that we shared so gratefully together. Both that gift of life and gift of love will never be cancelled but wonderfully completed. That tender love we experience will be genuinely transformed. Do you remember how our love expressed itself in the thought shared often—"It's just you and me." It didn't sound selfish then and it doesn't sound selfish now. In some special God-granted way it is still unchangeably true—it is still in some extra special way "just you and me." I love it so, and I will love you forever.

Love Always,
Lillian

*my joy*

# *I am with you*

## Dearest Lee,

All your life your temperament has made it so hard to accept change. Now it seems you are facing the most major change of your life. Everything for you has changed. I know you so well and sympathize so much. Remember, He who wisely and lovingly ordered the changes will guide you safely through them. This change for us was inevitable and there never would have been a "good" time to part. The change for me is all gain as promised, and that gain includes the hope of the re-gain of all we had together and much more. For you it must be much less, but do not fear. Nothing He has created that is good is lost. I've only reached home first. Your coming is lovingly expected. Take heart, dear, the change He has prepared for us will soon come to pass. No matter what changes, I am with you.

Love Always,
Lillian

*earthly goodbyes*

## Dearest Lee,

You visited today a dying patient in the hospital on the very floor where our earthly goodbyes were said not long ago. Your friend sadly will die without Christ or hope, even though he has often heard the gospel from you and others. We can hardly know the loss and misery of such a death. As you walked those hospital halls did you thank Him that from the hospital room I went directly home, the place prepared? It was not as we wished but as He willed. The days of doctors, surgeries, procedures and medications are now past. Would that all the hospital patients had such hopes as I. What the doctors' best efforts could not do, He has fully done. He has kept me vitally, happily, expectantly alive. Never see the hospital as a place of ending but rather the beginning of a brand new chapter of my life. The story continues, and you are and ever will be a part of it with me.

Love Always,
Lillian

28

## Dearest Lee,

How sad the words "others who have no hope." Yet, how gratefully do we embrace a hope unfading and undying that is placed in our risen, victorious and reigning Lord. How could our love be allowed to live on and hope allowed to die? Looking back upon our treasured past is written the saddening word "Nevermore." But upon our future is the gladdening word "Evermore." Christ's victory is our gift and is not deficient. It is total. Our Heaven is God's answer to suffering, sadness, shortness of earthly life and separation; all the work of a defeated enemy. He has not given us many particulars, only promises upon which we rest our hearts until all heartaches and heartbreaks be mended and ended. The form, the "how"—is not clearly disclosed but the fact of it is. Lee, let that fact be a refuge from all doubt and dismay. The answers to all your questions are sure to please you. Just trust Him; we never went wrong by trusting Him. "Evermore" is our word. Cling to it till all that's so certain becomes so clear at last.

Love Always,
Lillian

*treasured past*

## Dearest Lee,

You sweetly told me often that you did not think you could live without me. In the early days following my departure you felt that it was true. You could not so live. Don't even think of living without me. The "withness" is real, not imaginary. You don't have to live without me now or ever. Our weaving together by God in the marvelously mysterious oneness of marriage from God and in Christ is incapable of separation. It is God's blessing that we need never live without each other. Believe it fully, and let the fact of it bless your life during this painful interval in our love's story.

Love Always,
Lillian

*ysterious*

## Dearest Lee,

Tomorrow you will return to preach at the place where so much of our lives was spent in happy service for the Lord. If this for some reason will be your last sermon there, go into that pulpit tomorrow to thank Him in your heart for the privilege He gave us to do His work in that place. For forty years my prayers and my spirit were with you in your ministry. We will be together tomorrow as always. I want you to sense my presence with you. It will perhaps be our goodbye to a place where our love for the Lord and for each other flourished and grew.

Love Always,
Lillian

*for the Lord*

## Dearest Lee,

In love's beginning for us the dear Lord gave us a place in each others' heart. He gave us a treasured place in each others' life to live and love together through happy and fulfilling years. Now that we are separated in a temporary way, that place in each others' life will remain unoccupied fully until the place in our hearts which is made for only the two of us is filled again to be vacated never more. I will never be complete without you and you hopefully will not be complete without me. The two of us form one God-authored identity and He fully intends to stamp that identity with a permanence born of love, a love that lives and lasts. I love being identified with you, and I know truly that you feel the same about me. A Heaven-enkindled love is what we had, what we have, and what we shall have forevermore.

Love Always,
Lillian

*treasured place*

# *unfailing love*

## Dearest Lee,

Our love story is the result of the special love and grace of our Heavenly Father. He lovingly planned all of it before either of us was born. He designed every chapter of it far in advance. In due time, He graciously introduced each of us to His saving Son. In young and tender years He introduced us to each other and placed His love in us to mature and grow. The splendor of love we knew in our fifty-two years of "oneness" was possible only by virtue of His goodness and loving kindness. Even the inevitable earthly separation was dictated by an unfailing love. My removal meant glory for me but grief yet grace for you. Our love (His love) is intact. All He has been to us is true now, and the last chapter yet to be written, will only serve to prove that the gift of His love that made our story possible will not be removed, but rather restored in a way as yet unimaginable except to faith. Our love will not end in the suffering of separation nor the agony of absence but in a love that proves stronger by far than death. He meant it all along to be ours in Him forever.

Love Always,
Lillian

*fullness of love*

Dearest Lee,

The other day you experienced puzzlement and pain at the unexpected treatment of others. Great disappointment caused a deep hurt. You wanted so much to share it all with me, knowing that above all the others I would understand. I do understand and your hurts are somehow mine as they always have been. Lack of face to face communication does not for a minute mean that our two hearts are not in sweet communion with one another. I love you, dear, and I want that unfailing love to be your constant comfort. My love is not as great as His for you, but it is just as real because of Him.

Tell the sympathetic Savior about all your hurts because He cares more than all. But please tell me as well because I will know and understand. I am just in the next room, not far away. Someday we will tell each other everything and forever savor the fullness of love, caring and understanding where separation is unknown.

Love Always,
Lillian

## Dearest Lee,

How could we have possibly prepared ourselves for this unfamiliar phase of our lives? It did not really occur to us that life and love together was but a precious preface to a promised ending in the love of God. Our years in the splendor of partnership allowed little room for the thought that this union was of the nature of prophecy and promise with the very best yet to be. Had we but fully realized that Christian love has an eternal dimension, we would have invested more in that which would continue on after bodily separation. We believed firmly that our blending into one was the will of God from the start. Imperfect as the fulfillment of that will was done here during life's fleeting years, it will be completely done in Heaven. In Heaven, His will is done flawlessly. He who sovereignly determined this for us will wrap that oneness in wonder and prove to us endlessly that God still reserves the best for those who leave the choice with Him. I would choose a thousand times over His choice for me. You also have affirmed His choice often and today, as never before, we unitedly thank and praise Him for the love and wisdom that dictated it.

Love Always,
Lillian

*love and wisdom*

## Dearest Lee,

There is a sadness in death and parting which in some way is our sadness. Our indivisible oneness is a solemn fact and should cheer us immeasurably. When you come we shall be as we were on earth only in a much deeper, richer, fuller way. You have prayed that if it pleases our Father you might be able to love me more purely and honor me more fully than ever before. Your love and honor extended to me on earth was always deeply appreciated, and my response as ever now is to remember with gratitude and respond in love. It is true, "The Everlasting Love does keep us safe for each other whether there or here." I can't imagine that "without you" is in the will of God. Our happiness demands it and His love will provide it. I do believe that the blending by God of our two lives is too complete to be separated.

Love Always,
Lillian

*Everlasting Love*

*earthly experience*

## Dearest Lee,

Our union in marriage meant at last the end of long absences, during which our love for each other, planted there by God, grew and flowered. Marriage long-anticipated meant for us the end of separation and the beginning of a long togetherness with no forced goodbyes. This is what the coming reunion will mean for us, the end of separation and the beginning of a life of no parting—ever. Honeymoons are for knowing better and loving more. Why should not a new and wonderful phase of our life and love not begin with a "honeymoon" of knowing and loving beyond all earthly experience? He who created our love gives the best wine last.

Love Always,
Lillian

*object of affection*

Dearest Lee,

Our dear Lord has done great things for us whereof we are glad. He created marvelously and somewhat mysteriously a new identity, a new entity, a "we," an "us," a union, a seamless weaving together so each of our very persons themselves contains the other. He inspired the love that is the essence of our union. He increased our love and appreciation for that togetherness with every passing year. He insures our love against all losses, either here or there. I can joyously say that to die is gain in all things. Our love will be no exception. He who authored this oneness guarantees its preservation and perfection. Permanence is surely our hope for a God-ordained commitment and companionship. You often told me thankfully that forsaking all others was the most "right" thing you ever did and cleaving unto me the most rewarding. Cleaving there had its earthly limitations, but there are no limitations here. We are free to fully find out what this cleaving really means. Being the object of affection can only get better, far better.

Love Always,
Lillian

## Dearest Lee,

Today, June 5, 2003, is our 54th wedding anniversary. It is, not would have been, for what God did 54 years ago death cannot possibly undo. Beyond the earthly wedding ceremony He joined us in holy matrimony that is enduring. Jesus gave us the whole victory over death and that includes communion now and reunion after this temporary separation. Death is surely swallowed up in complete victory and our mortality is swallowed up in life. "Gain" awaits us; "better" is our future. We are still one in Christ. I will love you as long as He loves me, and that is forever. Today is our day, dear. I mark it thankfully and lovingly. You often wonder if I know how much you love me—I do know. Someday maybe soon I will be able to tell you so face to face, not just heart to heart.

Love Always,
Lillian

*heart to heart*

# savored and treasured

## Dearest Lee,

The Lord gave us so much happy sharing of the wonders and beauty of His creation. From the grandeur of the mountains to the glory of the sea His handiwork we enjoyed and enjoyed again. The sights and sounds of His beautiful world were savored and treasured. It is time again for our trip through the shimmering gold of aspens in autumn and the prospect of the Sierra Nevadas capped in snow. The same sovereign hand has prepared the place where I now dwell and wait for you. I say often as you do about me, "If only she were here and we could share all this wonder together as before." All these wonders, whether there or here, only grow lovelier in the sharing. I have much to show you. We will wander the paths and experience the joy made full, and thank the Father for a privilege renewed.

Love Always,
Lillian

## Dearest Lee,

All the loose ends of our life and love together have been left for you to manage without me—alone. I know how difficult some of them must be for you, as surely as others of them would have been for me had I been the one to remain. Those cares are ended for me but you must deal with a heart full of remembrances and a house full of reminders as a daily reality. To you, our home of so many happy years is now strangely empty and silent. Let us treasure all the God-given privileges and pleasures of our special home. I love you for all you are doing there on our behalf. Just remember dear why it is so painful now, because it was so precious then. There can be no suffering like the suffering caused by love, as our dear Lord knew better than all. The greater the love, the greater the pain and sorrow must be. He promises that this very sorrow shall be transformed into a joy which can never be taken from us. We eagerly await the fulfillment of our joy in reunion.

Love Always,
Lillian

*I love you*

*grace and mercy*

Dearest Lee,

My children and grandchildren are such a treasured part of my life even now. For so many years loving them and caring for them was always a delight and not a duty. My prayer continues to be that our family circle will be unbroken at last and the question doubly concerns me here—"Are all the children in at the end of life's day?" In Christ, in hope and in Heaven with us. I will meet you at the throne of grace and mercy and we will agree together as always for our dear children—to thank Him for what He has done for them and patiently wait for what He will yet do. I wish not to place an impossible burden on you but it would please me so much if, when you love them, you would love them a little extra for me. You have always thought that grandfathers are not nearly as adequate as grandmothers in so many ways. True or not, part of me stayed with you and may make it possible for you as father and grandfather to love them also in a motherly and grandmotherly way. This way I can still love a bit through you. Thank you dear.

Love Always,
Lillian

## Dearest Lee,

Think of me always as alive and real. Bring me vividly to your mind and heart as one who knows, remembers, loves, cares and waits. Love me as you always have because I am just away from you for a short season. We are united by our Father's loving will, joined by our Savior's loving hand. Our love is Heaven-born and Heaven-sent and will be Heaven-fulfilled. It is secured in Christ. We have had but the foretaste of love; we shall have the full taste of love. Meet me here...

> "Where the love that here we lavish on the
> Withering leaves of time
> Shall have fadeless flowers to fix on
> In an ever spring-like clime;
> Where we find the joy of loving
> As we never loved before
> Loving on, unchilled, unhindered
> Loving once and evermore."

Horatius Bonar
(1808-1889)

Love Always,
Lillian

*loving hand*

*gift of life*

## Dearest Lee,

I do know that doubts and fears about our future together arise in you from time to time and rob you of joy. We have nothing to doubt or fear. He is more than faithful who has promised. Unreality as to our Heavenly hope and home sometimes assault you and I have often seemed not only removed from your sight, but so very remote. It is then that your pain in our present separation is the most intense. Please know dear that I am much closer than you sometimes feel. My spirit, my mind and my heart are part of you and while vividly remembering, reach out to you in many ways. As long as you are there and I am here our communion, though unfamiliar, is still very real. The togetherness we've known is changed but not concluded. Our life and love as heirs together of the grace and gift of life eternal remains unsevered. He who is the author of it all affirms it still as being His will in the process of fulfillment and completion. Our love was sown and nurtured there over many years; the harvest is here and will be reaped joyously forever. He who would not allow even a suggestion of a tearing apart of what He had joined together will not permit a defeated enemy to do it either. Christ's victory over death is total, including separation. He secures our love against all loss.

A child often asks of a gift received, "Is it mine to keep?" Our loving Father/Giver assures us as His children that His gift of our love is ours to keep. This gift will not diminish. It will only grow more dear until its worth will be fully known and experienced. Let Him say to you always, "I will guard your treasure until you follow your heart home where your treasure is." We will thank Him together for all He has lovingly and faithfully done for us.

Love Always,
Lillian

gift received

*our life together*

## Dearest Lee,

Our love's story is now as always safely in the hands of its author. Our life together had a goal in a Risen Savior which could never be fully reached down there. It required a coming up higher, a coming home. Love interrupted is not love discarded. Everything God called good is promised a renewal, a restoration. I can tell you that what is still a largely undiscovered country to you is gloriously all right. Description would be lost in the very wonder of it all, but believe me it defies imagination. This is a cherished dream which definitely comes true. Remember, I am in your past in experience and memory but I am actually in your future. You will find me not in yesterday, but in tomorrow.

Until Then
Love Always,
Lillian

## Dearest Lee,

If you only knew. What we have known you and I of life and love should surely give promise that the best we have known in His grace can only be better in His glory. It is the lack of knowing all that lies before that at times must chip away at your trust and introduces fear in your heart. We used to sing, "If we could see, if we could know, we often say, but God in love a veil does throw across our way. We cannot see what lies before and so we cling to Him the more. Trust and obey, trust and obey." For me faith has given way to sight and I say to you quite confidently, "Take heart Lee, if you only knew." The sky of your hope would be cloudless, your fears faint and fading, your anticipation bright and shining. What I know now we shall know together one day and I can tell you so happily then, "Now you know."

Love Always,
Lillian

*now you know*

My dear fellow pilgrim on your way homeward through a valley unfamiliar and surely unwelcome...these expressions of my heart may seem to you but romantic notions or wishful thinking created by a lonely and lacerated heart. For two thousand years and beyond God's trusting people have entertained the hope and conviction that both life and love in Christ are wonderfully fulfilled and completed in our future home.

In early bereavement the pain of parting is intense, absence is an agonizing reality. There is a tender and tenacious desire to hold on to the earthly person, but that is not to be for death has separated what Christ in His total victory over death will unite in due time. He has faithfully guided His wounded child to focus increasingly on the now-heavenly person. Moving me away from what she was to me to what she is and ever shall be to me. She is truly no longer just a part of the treasured past but of the promised future. I love her for what she meant to me, what she means to me now and what she shall mean to me hereafter.

Charles Kingsley wrote in *Out of the Deep*: "I know that if immortality is to include in my case identity of person (it does) I shall feel for her forever what I feel now. The union I believe to be eternal as my own soul, and I leave all in the hands of a good God."

Job said, "...I was talking about things I did not understand, things far too wonderful for me." Job 42:1-6. I was tempted to utter these words about my thoughts on Heaven: its human, personal and relational character. This would be to deny Biblical revelation and the "revealings that were granted in asking, seeking and knocking." Many "concealings" remain but some glimpses, hints, perceptions and even careful speculations are granted to the sincerely searching heart. Many disclosures await the future. Those granted now, some of which are dim and only partial, are enough to allow Heaven's magnet to attract my heart. May He grant to you ample assurance for your badly broken heart.

These letters have been a sincere but inadequate way of telling our story with the hope that in the telling it might afford comfort to you who have said a tearful farewell to one irreplaceable person in your life. May it also convey the essential truth that all married love that lasts is triangular—husband, wife and Heavenly Father. Hopefully the Lord is the author of your life's story by faith in Christ and has authored your love's story as well. It will surely be a story of triumphs and tears, blessings and burdens, mountains and valleys and over all, the rainbow of His promise. To be in Christ and in love assures us that when the end of our story is reached here, we will truly live happily ever after. The saints of the ages have confidently believed that love from God and in Christ is stronger than death.

> "For love is as strong as death
> Many waters cannot quench love
> Nor will rivers overflow it."

Song of Solomon 8:6, 7

This word from John Watson in *The Upper Room,* 1895, is worth repeating: "There are a few fine souls who love once because they love forever, whose devotion is independent of sight, whose constancy deepens in absence…their love is an endless sacrament. But the impression grows dim on our world-worn heart, and would soon be effaced were it not for the magical resources of memory. The discovery of a letter will recreate the past and awaken slumbering emotions and vindicate the omnipotence of love."

Heaven's chief appeal for the Christian is "to be with Christ." That would seem to be all that is required, but it is not all that is revealed. I believe that loving relationships from God, in Christ, and based on a love greater than our own have a future beyond temporary interruptions. The loving Hand that joined us here will rejoin us there. That is my belief and my confident hope.

Lee Toms